LOVE *from* ABOVE

LOVE FROM ABOVE

ISBN: 979-8-218-91906-1
ISBN: 979-8-218-91907-8

www.vendelaraquel.com

Instagram @vendelaraquel
Instagram @anavah_collective

Woman & Rose Cover Art & Graphic Design
Hannah Battista

Hand & Rose Cover Art
Hannah Tremblay

Proofreading services
Priscilla Aguayo

Dedicated to Priscilla, Mona & baby Lola,
You 3 little ones are so loved and have brought massive joy
to our family. Thank you for your smiling faces.
It's been a blessing watching you grow.

Love,

Aunty Vendy

A poetry book crafted for women.

Designed to speak to the depths of a women's heart,
both young & old, for He makes us bold and whole.
It features ways my heart was warmed with both simple
and large joys. These poems are my personal testimony
as I sing praise in a lyrical way, describing how this
intimacy watered me. This love strengthened me during
the hidden battles that women fall victim to daily.
It details beauty I was too blind to see,
that slowed my heartbeat & transformed me.

May these writings bring your tender soul hope and
open eyes to everyday delights that bring light to life.
May it enhance your essence & infuse your life with
love from above.

November 11, 2019

Vendela, I will protect you from this world.
I hold you in the palm of my hand,
you rest on a bud of a rose and I will grow you.

The protection over your life is so strong Vendela.

I am doing something through and in you.
I created you and breath you to life.
Your life was a dream of mine and then I made you.

I am always watching you,
and you must know, my sweet daughter...
there is nothing you can not do.

From,

Your Love Above

LOVE

Love that works in mighty & small ways

Love that makes mountains leap

Love that plants an encouraging thought when you need it most

With me is gentle, soft, blissful love

Love so warm and soft,

like a blanket it wraps around your naked body on lonely and empty nights

Love that drops gentle truths in your mind

Truths that cut through lies

Truths that tenderize your little heart

With me is gentle, soft, blissful love

Love that ignites your senses to the beauty in each day

The true bliss that comes from a grateful heart

From eyes that see the rising sun

to a mouth that tastes the warm cup in your hand,

and skin that appreciates the warm water it rests in.

With me is gentle, soft, blissful love

In a world far from me,

I have made a way for all to drink in & be renewed by my tender

Love

GODLIKE

Beauty. Power. Strength. Compassion. Faith.

Through the crushing, through the pressing You have made me more divine

More Godlike

My understanding is pure

My heart is stretched

My view is vast

My labor is joyful

My love is authentic

My mind is true

The endured pain gave me wings to soar high, above the weight

I have been refined and made new

Through the crushing

Through the pressing

You have given me

Beauty. Power. Strength. Compassion. & Faith.

You make us divine

When we hand our pain over to You

We transform into something

Godlike

GLOW

There is no roller-coaster

No loss of appetite

No racing thoughts

No pain

No loss of sleep

The fear of what is to come

Rather

The warmth of the sun all over your body,

filling you from your head to
your toes

The cravings and taste of simple delights

The calm of your thoughts

The consistent love

The rest in your day

The excitement for what is to come...

Only You know how to make me glow from the inside out

The power to light my world and plant my dreams in a garden

filled with magenta & every shade of green

I choose this love

Please

Help me choose this love so everyday I

Glow

TREASURES

You give me treasures on earth
Warmth: hot coffee in the wind, mac & cheese that melts on my tongue
Butterflies: seeing the beauty in the setting sun EACH DAY
Honey: cream cheese frosting & baked goods, never letting go of my hand
Soothing: hope for today, hope for tomorrow
Your treasures are never ending,
they leave a trail each day and lead me back to You
You
My never ending stream
Overflowing with treasures
You
Are my
Heritage of blessings
Figures of Your grace lace my steps
Revealing blessings more plenty than the seeds of pomegranates
In the common places
I am still able to see Your treasures on earth
Forever, please be the keeper of my
Treasures

YOU

With a gentle whisper You make all better

Allow me to feel the joy in each day...

Open my eyes to the beauty

Hover over me with Your breath of life

Give me hope for the hour...

and what is to come

Protect against the fear and anxiety, the longing thoughts...

You

Sit by my side and warm me

My constant companion

I drink in Your hot cup of comfort each morning

Fueling my day & making a way

You

My dear Lord

My constant source of

Love is

You

ALL FROM YOU

The pale sand mountains make me feel tiny

Skyscraper palm trees surround me

Violet, burgundy, and tangerine flowers dance in the breeze

Webbed greenery crawls up the walls

Puffs of white line the baby blue backdrop

I take in the warmth from the sun and find rest

I breathe in the cool air

The beauty surrounds me once again but I only see it when I am still

When I am with You

You open my eyes

My eyes are open

You clear my lungs and slow my thoughts

I feel

I take in the rest

The peacefulness

Oh how You bless me

My sweet one

All from You

FROM YOU

Like a newborn
You held me close
Under your chest You
Grew me with Your milk
And protected my steps
Creating a gift
Of my life
The best
You give me
I still need Your milk
And to be held close each day
But I can now walk
And the way has been made
Your love was a shield
One that
Grew me tall
Grew me strong
Grew me wise
I drink in
The best
From You

YOUR CHOSEN ONE

You chose me

You formed me to know Your ways

But first

You chose me

You let in the morning rays

Fuel my days

Feed my Spirit

Water my garden

Open my heart

Comfort my mind

Keep me strong

Give me vision

Allow me to soar

Make me divine

I now know love

You showed me

To listen

To be truthful

To be kind

To surrender

To be patient

To be present

I can now love.

Love,

Your chosen One

REFUGE

Shelter

From the harmful thoughts

Painful deeds

Harsh elements

Injustice

You soothe my hurts with your Presence

I know You are enough

Your shelter is enough

It has never failed

Always taken care

Provided in the midst

More bountiful than before

Remember...

All I must do

When my heart starts to race

I go back to

You

Your shelter

You

My

Refuge

CREATION

The ocean is vast

The sand is plentiful

The sailboats wave in passing

The sun glistens off the horizon

I feel the earth beneath me

My bones lay heavy on its mantle

My toes sink into the cool sand

I hear the roar of the waves

I feel the sun's kiss on my bare skin

As I take in this view

You are with me

This beauty

For Your Creation

Freely available to all

To breathe in

The soothing state

The gentle calm

That comes from taking in

Your Nature

Your

Creation

PEACEMAKER

Thankful I fell first for Your...

Love

Like the soft breeze it

Comes at ease

Only You...

So powerful

Your silence brings me peace

Great peace

You fill all my visions

My sky

My heart

My plans

My future

You

My first love

My peacemaker

Each morning

You take me to the top of Your mountain

The view is grand

The climb is light yet

One I could not do without

You

Each morning

You make a way

For Your divine ways

Water me by

Filling me with truths

I did not know & needed to know

I need

Me

Forever needing

My waymaker

My

Peacemaker

DELIGHT

You my delight

Delight me

With the desires

Of my

Heart

Restful nights

Peaceful mornings

Kisses from the sun

Iced matcha

Tunes to lift my soul

Silk on my skin

Vibrant colors out my window

Violet painted nails

Hope for the day

Excitement for

You

You who loves to...

Bless me with

Delight

UNIVERSE

Only You can be my

Earth

Moon

Sun

&

Stars

You center me

My confidence

My expectations

My desires

My beliefs

You exceed all things

Only You can carry that weight

Only You can keep afloat my ways

Temptation for others to do this

Will be there

But I will always know

It's only

You

Who moves my axis

It's only

You

Who rotates

My

Universe

LET ME

In your presence

You love me

You love me so well

You cast away lies

Unfold truths

Harvest vision

Your presence is

gentle, peaceful, not of this world

The cloud is soft, like a marshmallow

I sit high in the sky, a view from above

The earth is far from sight

It's there where You fill my cup to the top

I have enough for the day

Tomorrow will come

But for now

It's just You and I

I am now ready for what is next

Next in the hour, Next in the moment, Next as I sit

I do not understand, the closer we grow, I do not understand

Your ways, So simple

And yet

I fail time & time again

Take my heart, take my mind

And make it Yours

I will try to let You...

Your goodness in

I will try to let You

Love Me

In your presence is where

I let You

Love Me

In You

Let Me

LIGHT MY CANDLE

You lay me down
Slow my heart
And spirit
My comfort comes when
You Light my candle
You fill the atmosphere
It burns effortlessly
Giving light to all who enter the room
The flame moves up and down with ease
A simple doing with Mighty results
You Light my candle
Its fragrance fills a room with bliss
The light is dim and soothing bringing peace to the present
Flooding with
Great simplicity & Mighty Joy
All
Comes from You
Who knows how to
Light my Candle

TIME

The leaves fade
The flowers fall
Minutes pass
Turning into hours
Days full come sunfall
One foot in front of the other
One step at a time
Then comes
Light for the next
Never two at a
Time
My forever guide
What You have opened
No one can shut
But help me stay
On Your path
The road
Filled with signals and such
Help me be awake
Create a hunger in me
I can not shut
The time will pass
But as long as I have You
There is no worry
I just need our quality
Time
Vision for the future
More vast than I could ever
The greatest things are yet
The journey is long
But You are at my side
One step
At a
Time

CHOICE

Your love
Sun after sun
Moon after moon
Day after day
Has showered me in truth
Guiding my
Daily
Choice
Your love is filled with
Truth so
Honorable
Just
Pure
Loving
Excellent and...
Praiseworthy
You establish my each step
Saying this way
Turn right
Turn left
My heart yearns
To keep Your commands
Because I know
I have experienced
Your
Love
A love so strong
I am empowered
To choose You
Everyday
With my
Choice

HEART

My eternal

Your unchanging nature brings comfort to

My heart

You lead me down long paths filled with

Honey

Warmth

Kindness

Lavender

Joy

Sunsets

Rest

Friendships

Peace

Family

Homemade nut milks

Sun kissed skin & more

On this path

The fruits are abundant

I taste and feel all I see

My heart

On this path

Warms & Grows

It experiences affection

On this path

You decide who enters

My heart

I find comfort in

You

Whose ways are

Eternal

When you hold

My

Heart

NEW

The suffering was made durable
The waves are calm
The mountain tops are steps away
The fear is now
Gone
The night turns to day
But I now see Your
Moonlight
Lit the
Way
I now feel the sun
I now have peace
The pain is at
Ease
Time & time again
You make new the old
And the old becomes
New
Endless possibilities are
With You
Hope that comes
New

WHOLE

You
Unleash the streams
Streams from above
Washing over the wounds
You cause a
Flow
Filling the
Holes
Making me
Whole
I tell of Your goodness
You Who
Enjoys blessing me
With little things
With large things
With simplicity
With complexity
With wonder
With child-like eyes
With grace that
Overflows
Feeds me and others
To
Grow
With gifts that point to the
Stars
With gifts that flow from the
Heavens
You light
The moments of my life with joy
Making me
Whole

ME

You see what my eyes can not

You know what I do not

You are before me

You are after me

You exist in ways I do not

You never stop

So I believe You

When You say

"It's done, Trust me"

Comfort for the present

Is all I need

I place my faith in You

Your best

Is done with

Me

My sweet love

In me You create

Mighty faith

Trusting You

For each step

Not all that is

Next

Mighty faith built on believing all I do not see

But whisper to me

My Almighty

Grow in me

Mighty faith that

Gives peace

Peace to know

It's done

By You

Who is with

Me

DANCE

Protected are Your words
That grow in my heart
Soothing my mind
Allowing me to live free, causing me to
Dance
Your words freely given to all You love
Live in those who seek You and find You
From this You create a masterpiece
*A soul that is a **KISS** to the world*
Kindness flows from them
Inspiration is what they exhale
Soothing other tired, hurt souls by
Seeing the truth planted in their roots
Your kiss is what opened my mind
Creating in me a masterpiece
Under Your branches You grow me close
Your watchful eye never leaving my side
Growing my each step You light all I see
I am Your masterpiece
Like a tree, rooted to the ground Your leaves grow tall
Providing all who rest under Your tree with shade
There is no uprooting Your stance so I will
Dance
Under You, my forever tree
The shade is free, for all who then enter through me
As You keep watch with a close eye I will
Dance
under Your branch
Because their is no uprooting Your shade filled stance
Yes, I will continue to
Dance
All my days, and water Your stance with joy
You, my mighty tree Who allows me to
Dance

HONEY

I come to You each day
I feel the warmth of Your hug
As You hold me close
Your love sweetens my day
And out of me flows
Honey
This honey from You
I never want to forget
I must taste it each day
Not only is it sweet
But pure
Untouched
Rare
Oh so unique
It's delightful
It brings flavor to all
And it's mine each day
I will taste the honey today
Watch it soak all it touches
This honey is from You and me
It's what we make together
And it will set me free
Free from the worry, free from the doubt
Free from the chains that chased my days, free from the drought
This honey is sticky
It's the glue for You and me
It keeps my life sweet
So please
Continue to make new honey with me
The passing rays display
It's the greatest gift
And brings much comfort to me
You my sweet
Honey

MY WAY

Today You gave me a glimpse of

My way

Due to the easy mornings with You

That comes so free

Shining rays from the sun

Slip into my space

And You fill it with grace

To light my day

Peace & calm, violets & plum

New life so powerful and strong

Will be the way

You create for me

You,

Who has set me free

My path is set

Straight will be

My way

Pain will enter but it does not have to stay

For with You

I have the power to turn the lights on

And when the light comes

Darkness's only choice is to flee

It has no space

No power to fill my days

For with You My path is set straight

You have already made a way

I will rest up and take in

These sunny days

Okay

For I know

The beauty and wonder is

You are always with me

Lighting

My way

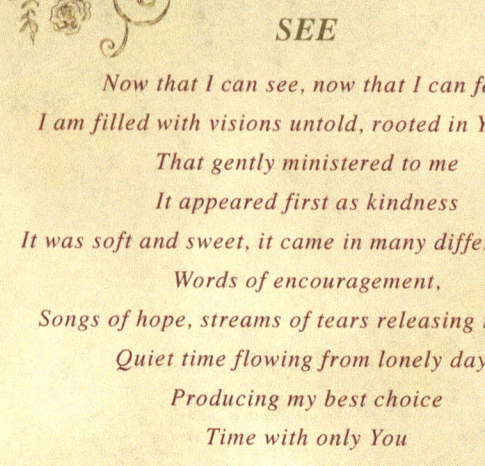

SEE

Now that I can see, now that I can feel
I am filled with visions untold, rooted in Your love
That gently ministered to me
It appeared first as kindness
It was soft and sweet, it came in many different forms
Words of encouragement,
Songs of hope, streams of tears releasing the fears
Quiet time flowing from lonely days
Producing my best choice
Time with only You
There we took
Walks in Your creation, day in and day out
Thoughtful flowers and notes helped to remove the doubt
The pain of the day
Which I now know was never meant to stay
But to grow me, bond me to You
My forever root
Your gentle ministry moved mountains
Lifted my branches & grew me
Free from the bending and pleasing
It directed my steps, carved names in my heart
Made it so I could not lead without You
But rather trust with every ounce
May Your love rain first in my heart
You Who helps me
See
Your gentle ministry
Poured down like the rain
It ran with no limits & fulfilled my every need
I am so thankful for You, my sweet love
For Your daily feed and making a way
So I can now
See

WOMEN

Powerful & tender

Beautiful & kind

Gentle & strong

Loving & so divine

So easily consumed by a man

Why Father? I don't understand

Show me Your plan, help me understand

You tell

"To trust Me"

To set me free because

The design is different

You are my vine

And oh so divine

Your strengths may be different

But not to worry all you must do is

"Trust in me"

The fruit will cause blessings

To be set free but please do not allow

My feelings to grow unless You are

At the center of my every sow

You scatter my seeds & water what needs

Please Father, take my needs

And show me the way, so others can see

Your divine Creation

Is Your Spirit living in me

So today make a way

And set free all Your caring, loving

Mother's to be

Show us the fruits

Of the gardening that takes place

The colorful life that flows

From all of Your

Women

LEAVE

I just want to know

How to love You

The most

When I love You most

When You come first each day

The pain fades away

The comfort is abundant because You never change

You are my most consistent love

One that will never

Leave

I know this because I experience it

Everyday

And You are the source

That drives my day

You always

Making the way

Things may fall apart

But I will always have You

And like the passing of each day

Certain things will always stay

You will always be here

To greet me and show me the way

So please

Grant me excitement

Because

This I know

This I believe

But also help me understand

The Peace

That should flow

From knowing You

Will Never

Leave

NEEDS

My needs are met

With our silent time together

There I am taken care of

You uncover the lies

Open my eyes

In silence is where my heart lies

In silence

You serve a cup of warm tender love

Overflowing with comfort

To prepare me as You meet all my

Needs

In silence

I hear Your creation sing

I wake with the earth

And feel the butterflies in my tummy

It's just You and me

"Now come, and sit with me"

In silence I sit

Out my window I see

The lush green and skyscraping palm trees

One day this view is sure to change

But for now I'm just so grateful for

My view with You

In silence

You teach me Your ways

They are so humble and fill me with amaze

I do not understand the life of Your

Lamb

But I will try to follow His lead

Grow the silence in me

Destroy the doubt

Because in silence lies the answers to all my

Needs

SHEEP

I may never understand

The way You mold me in Your hand

Your goodness

Your sweet love

The way You care for me

I do not understand

Your mighty plans

But make me into Your gentle

Sheep

I may never understand but I plan

To give You my human

Life, Soul, All I have

May each day be filled with Your ways

You, my never ending root

My rest

My peace

My love

I, Your

Sheep

I never want to leave Your side

Your mighty ways are just too divine

You lift me creating freedom in

All I see

Thank You, my sweet One

I wake this morning with

Full, bubbling, overflowing

Gratitude

For You

The One I will always choose

I may never understand but I plan to give You all I see

For there is abundant freedom when I abide in You

All I understand, all I plan, I lay it at Your feet

For I am Your gentle

Sheep

FLY

You

Make my yoke

Light

The load may not

But you carry

Me

You hold me

Tight

Please my

Dear one

I love You

I just want You

Who loves me right

Who makes me light

You who carries my tired soul

You who makes me

Full

Please my

Dear one

Today don't leave my side

For it is only You who I want

Only You

Who makes the journey

Feel like less of a fight

Only You my

Dear one

Who can make me

Fly

ROAD

You take me on Your path

The scenery is beautiful

Mountains so tall

Oceans so vast

Rivers that flow

Valleys so low

Colors so vibrant

Fragrance that flows

You hold my hand & whisper which way to go on this road

You lead me down paths I am too weak to go

You take me to new heights

I could have never on my own

Much happens on this road

The weather changes

The people come and go

The direction is not always clear

But You never seem to fail

And always tell me the way to go

I love traveling down Your road

You lace it with blessings I could have never

On my own

This morning I hear the rain but

I no longer feel any pain

I will go where You want me to go

I will love who You want me to love

I will do all You want me to do

I will stay on Your road

Just hold me close

My dear guide

And never leave my side

For this path

I do not want to leave

I will always journey on Your

Road

LOVE

It pours out

Big apple red

Warm, soft & never ending

It goes down smooth

It's pure, it delights in truth and healing

It journeys high, wide

It flows, makes me glow

From the inside out

Oh You

I need more to consume my mind

Drown my seconds

Minutes, hours & days

Touch every moment & awake me to You

Your never ending

All consuming supply

Sweet

Gentle

Kind

Strong

Pure

And always

New

Only You

Your love

I will keep it close as it supplies

All my needs

Desires, wants, and truths

It's You I need

Your

Love

FOREVER TRUE

Close are You to my thoughts, to my heart
Even when my mind drifts
I still find You close to me
I want You to come first
In my mind & heart
I must know how
Teach me how
To keep You first
I must know, show me how
To surrender to You my
Forever true
I have grown tired
Tired of doing it on my own
Restless in the state of the unknown
So I surrender
The movement grows fluid
Oh so effortless
You teach me how to trust in You for each step
I love the way You show me
How to surrender my all to You
Surrender brings peace
Surrender is not defeat
But when met with ease
Lifts the clouds away
And makes a way
Brings comfort to the unknown & overthrows the throne
Of worry and hurt, pain and grief, loss and suffering
Soothing my soul,
You teach me the power, the need in
Moments with You filled with truth
I find my rest
And surrender my best
To You my
Forever True

LOVE ALONE

By love & love alone
You have directed my steps
Through winding and twisting roads
The mundane of the day drifts away
The confusion in the mist
Pounding heart and racing thoughts have no lift
By love & love alone
You have directed my steps
Simply put it is Your ways
By love & love alone
That carve the philosophy of my heart
Trusting with each step
A challenge I never seem to forget
Yet
Your promises
Great and faithful
Raise my every step
One after the other
My leg will lift
And with every promise
I see in time
The beauty outshine
The suffering
That has no more
Rise
Greater are You
By love & love alone
Your ways
You
I will always follow
By Your
Love Alone

DIVINE

Much I do not see
But You see it all
I have parts, You have the whole
As a result when I give in to You
My forever true
I can choose a higher way
Decisions bearing fruit
I know my view is not bad, it's just not
All knowing
All seeing
All powerful
My sweet One
I enjoy the view with You
Your cloud of rest
Grants wisdom and helps me decide
From a view I normally do not abide
A view that is omnipresent
A view from You my
Omnipotent
The choice is always mine
But I'd rather look to You
My divine
Your ways never lead me astray
But fill my heart so I can obey
With You all comes full circle
As I rest on Your cloud, fill my view
So I can make decisions
That come from
Trusting in You
My rest
My shelter
Where the wisdom lies
In the cloud of the
Divine

DAY

It is You
Who has brought me this far
So it is You I will trust in
You Who fills my life with blessings of the mind
So true in their design
Simply thought
And then You provide
I will look to You
And remain worry free
You My moon and stars
All I see
So again
I will look to You
And be worry free
Nothing can rob my peace
Because You are always with me
I will wait patiently for You
To do what only You can do
My garden is in bloom
Even under the moon
Bountiful and full
Fresh fruits are on the way
To lace each
Day

UNTOLD

It is now Time

The tide was high, it has now subside

My love, it is time

To reap blessings of many kinds

That shine as bight as the sun

Are more vast than the ocean, and as pure as snow

These blessings will flow from souls

Who have journeyed through the most

With stories untold,

The souls that walk close to You

Know all things happen in Your time

The night does not last

The glory outweighs the pain

The old becomes new

It is time because You are good, faithful

And Your nature is kind

You love to forgive & then

Give

To the souls that belong to You

Come blessings and treasures so true

They have looked to You to provide their every need

Now it is time

For You to do what only You can do

So I will sit and watch the vines reach high

To the sky

I will watch the roses bloom and the birds sing

I can now feel the butterflies, in Your land

The milk & honey

It comes from heavens design

It pours out with streams of life

I will watch the eyes stare in delight

Because it is now time for a move of the divine

For the Mighty in the stories

UNTOLD

SHADE

Saved from the world
Speedy & empty
Shut eyes & meaningless linger
From the spinning
Now Shade covers me
Under a palm tree I see
Simplicity of all sorts
Beneath the shadow lives
Thoughtfulness in a note
Thank yous that travel so far
Tender blueberry scones
Under the desert sun
Tiled roofs, clay arches
Burgundy and lime
Coffee with a view
Glowing skin
Pink tops
Fluffy puppies
Stretchy pants
Lemon trees
With palms that reach
Out numbering my gaze
The peaceful days
Cause my lungs to expand
With gratitude open my eyes to
Chandelier skies
Beauty so divine
It follows Your every move
And those who dwell close to You
See, feel, taste
And enjoy
The beauties under Your
Shade

RUN

Run
To You
When the confusion is in my midst
And the pain gains
I run to You
The harsh winds that blow
Carry me to You
This is why
All things happen
For a reason
You the master weaver
Use it all for good
Even the times
I do not understand why
You gently reveal
The unknown
And bring the calm
Under Your song
I will always praise
Your name
And run to You
Far and wide
Keep whispering Your truths
To get me through
They are all I need
In times of plenty
And dry
To You I
Run

CAN'T DO

Nothing You
Can't do
Time & time again
You bless me with the best
Rest of the soul
Creating a sound mind
Peace in the unknown
As I cling to You
Delights lace my day,
Wonder around the corner
Hope for all to come
Joy for the moments at hand
Love in relations I have no control
It is You and there is nothing You
Can't do
I tell of Your glory
Because of the freedom
It has brought to me & all I see
The mountains have moved
The climb...oh how it grew
But only You knew my needs & now I know
There is nothing You
Can't do
May the world see
The majesty You bring
To a life
Lived true by You
May all the eyes see & the ears hear
Your footprints in the life
Of those that care for You
Your Creation
Your truth
My Dear
There is nothing You
Can't Do

FROM YOU

How do I know
How do I discern
What is of and
From You
My mind fills with
Thoughts, desires, dreams
All sorts of things
But how do I know
What is of and
From You
I try to create time and space
To be still and meditate
Then I ask
You and
Your Son
What is truth
What is
From You
The things
Beautiful, wonderful, mysterious things
You tell me
The how and why
Then peace fills my mind
But now I know what I must do
It's simple
All I must do is trust You for the fruits
And down will flow
All that is
From You

FEEL

I feel warm

I feel light

I feel the sea breeze

At peace

I feel whole

When my body is still

I feel Your love

Covering my life

Causing me to

Feel

With You

There is no end to the love I

Feel

How I must be with You

Each day to

Feel

Free & Calm

I never knew how beautiful it is

To feel with my heart, mind & soul

When I feel I experience You

Your creation, Your nature, all that is good and true

My true, I love You

I will feel today because it will not stay

The lessons are new please just keep me close to You

Then I can do all You'd like me to do

You keep me alive, cause me to thrive

It is by You, I am new

I feel the day & as it passes away

I look to You to keep pure

All I do

Oh how I love the way You make me

Feel

GREET

I struggle

To see from Your view

My thoughts get muddy

My mind wonders

I am fixed on things I should not

You help me

You make a way

To show up and

Greet

All that meets me today

The good, the blessings, the work I see

That lies before me

Help me be faithful

Help me be strong

So I can stay on Your path, I know the time will pass

And as I look to You

I want my heart to be true

So do what You have to do

Make me new

Keep my sight fixed

Fill me & carry me through,

keep me true,

I will always love You

I thank You for this day

For tomorrow the wind may blow

The unknown at my feet

But I promise it is You

I will always wake to

Greet

RENEWED

I may try but I always fall short
You however are greater than
The hurt
The pain
And any shame
You cover & make all right
You tell me this today
So I can move forward
With expectations so true
There will be hurt, there will be pain
Because all are not You
But Your ways have paved
It set the bar
Cleared the clouds
Opened hearts
And made
New
Love from You
Is patient
It accepts delays
Problems and sufferings
Free from anger
It's kind in nature
Gentle and smooth
There is no envy
False desires of others
No boasting with pride
Your love is tender
Not proud
It knows no agenda
But rather a limited self
There are no records of wrongs
Life close to You is to live
Renewed

NEVER LATE

Never late
But slow with me
Quick to wait
Kindness is what You breathe
There is much I do not see
But patience is what You breathe
With each rising sun You speak to me
Words I need to encourage me
To stay on Your path
To trust in Your timeline
For all I see
This I can do
This I enjoy
Because You are close to me
Time and time again
Your faithfulness leads me
To my desires & dreams
Never late, always on time & patient with me
I will trust today because it is You who
Makes the way
Your peace is what feeds me
Today I will be on time for You
For there is not a moment where
You are ever late, no not one
Because You are
Never Late

NEW WINE

The need to believe
The need to let go
Of the disbelief
In order to taste the new wine that flows
Now is the time,
Ripe & ready
Through the crushing & the pressing
Came new vines
Time to drink & enjoy
The labor under the sun that flows from
The new skins within
A gift from You, I can now see
By death, my cup was tipped, that was it
A season filled with restless nights, weary mornings & sleepy days
It was there You met me & now I know the necessity
Of the new wine that flows from within
Time to drink, time to enjoy
The cup You have prepared for me
So erase my disbelief, lower my walls & let in the love
You wish to stay
Let it fill my life as I look to You
I wake with open eyes & a heart that desires
Truth for You & all You do
The signs are there as You
Wake me with each rising sun
I am greeted by Your love
Your joy is planted in me, I have the power to live free
Now that my greatest care is to dwell close to You
I will experience wonders that could only be from You
The Creator of all, the Almighty
Truly there is nothing You can't do
2.25.21 for today marks
A season & time filled with
New Wine

LIFE

So unique

Does not operate in this time

It will travel far & wide

A soul that powers over the flesh

Yes , rare to find but You

Create humans & make them divine

You feed my spirit

So it can go the distance

The desires of my heart

Must not compare to my desire for

You, my One & Only true

New is on the horizon

Truth is paving the way

Helping hands are there & so is Your love

A breakout of Your spirit

The sound of sweet victory is near

This is due to the darkness that once surrounded me

It was there where I grew to handle all You brew

The time is near because it was

You Who held me close when no one could

You Who gave me hope when no one could

You Who promised beauties that watered my soul

When I could not hold the pieces of my heart

You see it was You Who made me whole

Now I am ready to give You my life

For with You I lay down my life

To gain a life from You

This life will point to You

This life is from You

This is the beginning of my

New life with You

For it was You Who laid down Your life

To give me

Life

DESIGN

Coffee walks

Writings

Music & Sunshine

Sleep

Family talks

Friends

Care for my

Hands & feet

Plants & trees

Beach days & good reads

Kitchen time with meal design

Clean & organized

Ready for the week to be

Sundays are rush free

Rest

Coffee

Let the praise be

Slow & steady

Calm & present

Oh how You bless me with weekends of my dreams

Bubble baths & wine

FaceTimes with time

I wake ready for the work ahead

Time to think and be

Happens on my weekends

From You they stem

I love to create with time

&

Rest, Rest, Rest

All part of your master

Design

SEE

I want to live a life
Full of Your spirit
Your cotton candy skies
Your gentle care
Your kind words
Your strength
Your forgiveness
Your light yoke
Your morning delights...
Birds chirping out my window
Iced coffee with fresh nut milk
Healing words
Simple truths
Bubbling gratitude
Pineapple lamps
Egyptian moon candles
Green plants
Heating pads & cozy socks
A life filled with Your spirit
Births greater views with each passing moon
As a result I have all I need
The rest is shade
That comes from the trees
You plant close to me
In my mind & my heart
There will never be a day
I do not praise You for all You have done for me
With each passing moon I see
How real your glory should be
For all the world to
See

MOLD ME

Hold me
Form me
Mold me

Make new
What only
You can
Do

My flesh is weak
My mind is willing
The bruises will heal
The faithfulness
Rooted
Will prevail
I choose
You

Hold me
Form me
Mold me

Do what only
You can do
And make me new

Hold me
Form me
Mold Me

SUNSETS

New life
Rings in as I start to enjoy
The days under Your sun again
You make Your sunsets follow me
Everywhere I go
To the ends of the earth
These sunsets, they will flow
And rays of light will stem from my life because I will
Always follow Your sunsets
To the ends of time Your sunsets are a sign
May they never leave my life
May they always warm my heart
And make me smile
Days and dates with You
May the sign of the sun remind me of You
Your never ending goodness that starts new & ends each day
May many of my days under Your sun
Be filled with sweet moments with just You
It is You my love Who plants the seeds
If I fall into the wrong hands it's You that will understand
And lead my heart back to You
All I can do is thank You
For showing me what it is to love
Time and minutes with You
For they will pass but Your love
It grows new & more
With the sunsets I will reflect
On Your love I deeply fill in the sea breeze
And wisdom oh it flows
I might never experience more joy than in this moment with You
But I promise to follow You & Your sunsets
That bless me with rest and pleasures so true
Nothing will compare to quality time with You
May I always follow You & Your
Sunsets

DESIRE

It is You Who planted

My every desire

Rooted in You

Is all that is

Good

The time has come because You made me new

Now the desires will follow me

I can no longer follow them

My sweet One the desires are following me

Because I choose to follow You

The desires are real they kept me going

But were not the reason for my survival

The desires are real

And the ones from You

Lead me on a path filled with doors

Opened by You

Thank You for the desires

I just ask that

They never become

Stronger than

My desire

For

Just

You

For You are my greatest

Desire

TRUST

I find the more I trust
The better You are able to take the lead
I trust in You
Your ways
Higher than my ways
Your thoughts
Higher than my thoughts
They are what sets me
Free
The more I trust
The greater the picture
You paint for me
The more I trust
The more I am
Free
I can wake to greet each day
Full of mystery
For it is You
Who leads me to meadows
And down sunny paths
I am relaxed and stress free
I am full and energized
Because it is You who
Leads the way and points my each way
My heart overflows with gratitude for You
And because of this I have bliss
Each day trusting more and more
In Your will that lights my way
I pray with each passing ray
I grow closer to You and Your ways
May I always be filled each day because in You I place my
Trust

VIEW FROM ABOVE

My eyes are not fully open

Because I do not have a

View from above

You see

The view from above

Comes when I seek

You

When I spend much time

With Your spirit

When I pray

And wait for

You

Your words

Your thoughts

Your moves

Your love has surrounded me

As a result

You desire to bless

In mighty ways

The way You

Can now

So help me fully

Experience

The peace

Under

Your sun

As I continue to seek You and Your

View from Above

THIS MOMENT

The morning will pass
And so will the moments we have
People will go
Excitement will flee
Disappointment will come
But through all this
It is still You Who is with me
I may become easily consumed but I know
It must always be You at my root
Everyday my reason to praise
Is from this love from above
That will never leave
You might look away
Withhold from me
When I fail to swallow truth
But
Today I praise
Not for all to come
Or all that was
But for this moment
And the moments I just have
You
My guide, my light
My never-ending source
Of all that is good
It is You who feeds my soul
I wake with faith due to spending time with You
It renews for all I must do
I will keep the faith & trust in only You
Because all I need to get through is this moment with You
Please multiply
This Moment

WELCOME

Faithful one

Chosen one

All from You

The sun

The tunes

As I rest under the palm trees

And bask in the golden light

I know You

Are always by my side

The glow

It's You

The sunny rays

The ocean breeze

It's You

My peace

My love

My full heart

It's You

The vibes that lie on my heart

Are all from You

If only I open my eyes

And stay close to You

I love You

I am here

And I will welcome

Your music

Your vibes

All my

Life

Near me, all my life, always are You

Welcome

BELIEVE

I know what it is I must do
Trust You in all I do
And not all I see or feel
For feelings can be laced in deceit
The joys are all from You
Never have You steered me wrong
So why do I live with such disbelief
Might it be the deceit that lives in me
My flesh
But truly I know it is You my guide
Always by my side
Who helps me do
All I need to
So help me believe
And live in great peace
Knowing what flows in and out of my life is all from You
Today I will rest and drink in Your sweet comfort
Because it allows me to take my next step in the midst of disbelief
Truly I know
Your comfort will
Always be with me
For this is what I need
Please help me
Believe

PEACE

The sound of palm trees
Touching in front of me
Stillness
Awareness of You
With cold toes
Under cozy sheets
Wrapping me
As I sit and seek
Listen & Wait
Love grows near
It's in people I see
This is a blessing
To wish only
Peace
For those that walk the land
Because of this
I see so differently
I want nothing but the best
For Your people
Even the ones that hurt me
Oh how much
Peace
This gives me
To live close to You
Your peace is what holds me
The look, the sound, the feel
Pure tranquility, peace with You
Is what I need to surround me
All my days please pour over me Your
Peace

BLINDFOLDS

Our time
Under the passing suns and moons
Creates strongholds that blindfolds....
The blindfolds over my eyes
Were from living in a world far from You
Blinded to Your truth
When I was little I felt You near
Your spirit & truth
It was what guided me and as I grew
This world far from You consumed
Chipped away at me
Yes, there is much to enjoy
But none of the pleasures
Last without You
A lack of You and Your truth
Creates empty space even the greatest of blessings
Can't consume
Now I am back
I see things from Your view
View from above
My senses have been made new
I am no longer blind to the divine
That lifts my each step
As a result I am renewed
Restored to my childlike view
Before this world influenced my thoughts
But it is now You Who guides in what I do
So much goodness
Flows from Your truth & we experience new life with You
When all is removed & lifted from my eyes is the disguise that blinds
Thank You for doing what only You can do
Keep going, never stop removing the
Blindfolds

YOU & YOUR WAYS

When I do right by You

I have peace

There is safety in

You & Your ways

Never do they lead me astray

Your love preserves

In ways unheard

You are

Honest

Gentle

Kind

Patient

Just

Loving

I'd like to be more like You in all I do...

Honest, gentle, kind, patient, just and loving

I'd like to be more like You

When I am like You

I am worry free

Because I know tomorrow will take care of itself

And there is plenty for me to greet

In the present day so as I learn from

You & Your ways

I will trust You are enough with each passing ray

May I always choose

You & Your Ways

EACH DAY

Simplicities lace my day

In them You plant joys of all sorts

Restful nights

Early mornings with the sun

Singing birds

Warm coffee

Fluffy robes

Scented candles

Devotionals

Writings

Cozy socks

&

Stillness

I love to wake

With Your rising sun

There You meet me each day

Pouring hope into all I see

Giving me wisdom & strength

It's new each day

It's now something I crave

The crashing of waves will never sway

Me from Your tender ways

Because I have learned to lean on You

All my days

The calm is near

Nothing that can't be done

Now that You are here

I just want to say

Thank You for cultivating

A desire for You as I wake

Each Day

BEST

When I see the brokenness around me
I look to You
It is in the cracks Your love is showcased
Best
I see the pain of humanity
The abuse of power
The lack of wisdom
The lies they believe
However, it is in the cracks Your love is showcased
Best
The misuse of power saddens me
It is not the design You created us to be
The lack of wisdom that flows from deceit
Makes the desires of the flesh run free
Causing pain to all who conceive
Planting lies in her & all she sees
However it is in the cracks
Your love is showcased
Best
Like a flood Your love travels
It covers the cracks healing the shattered cracks
In this flood is light & wisdom
Truth that delights
So please
Release Your flood on all I see
I enjoy watching the flood fill the cracks
Over the brokenness that stems
From Man & Woman
Adam & Eve
May it move without boundaries
And overpower all it sees
For it is in the cracks
Your love is showcased
Best

DAILY REMINDERS

These You give me

Daily reminders of all I need

You

Truth from You

Gratitude for all that's done & yet to come

When I start my days with You

These three things bring peace

And help me believe

They fight the battle against disbelief

Through the ups and downs

They ring in victory

Your promises give me life

I lost what

Only I could gain with You

New life

How good

The more I learn of your status

Even the highs and lows

Are no match for the

Daily reminders

You give me

May more of Your creation inhale these custom and oh so true

Daily Reminders

OCEAN WAVES

Beach days with sounds of ocean waves
A peaceful scene is what You give me
Toes in the sand
Shut eyes & kisses from the sun
The water & the ocean
The sea
It speaks to me
Calms my world & soothes my mind
Rest of the best I find
Near Your sea breeze
With the sound of Your waves
The worries & stress wash away
The sun is seated high
And keeps a close eye
On all that lives
Under its daily rise
Thank You for this time
In this
Creation of Yours
I will find rest
To the sound of
The ocean waves that fill my days
May I never lose sight of the
Beauty, healing & rest
That washes over me
When I just sit and be with Your
Ocean Waves

ENOUGH

You help me see

The beauty in the journey

Enough

Is what You give me

Why is this important to see

My worth in Your eyes

My being

My doing

Is enough

For You

Enough for

You

Must be

Enough

For me

So thank You

For creating in me

A sound mind

Knowing

For

You

I am

Enough

CAREFREE

It's the way You take care of me

There are reasons to worry

But it's the ways

You have always showed up

The many ways You love me

As I sit & sip my soup

And take in this view

Under the moonlit sky I feel the sea breeze

And heat lamp that rest close to me

The soup goes down smooth

Aware I am of the many ways I enjoy

Sitting with You, deep in me You created

A desire & the more it grew

The closer I became to You

My lifeline

My love so true

Help me always follow You

Not because all You do

And the many ways You make new

But due to the nature of only You

Only You can take care of

Your creation in a way that makes them new

Only You can take care

So first let me be held by You

Together may we experience

Many more moments of truth

Under Your moon more waves & carefree days

I do not know what tomorrow may hold but the trust

You are growing in me allows me to be

Carefree

SEASON

In this season

Every minute, every hour, every second

You want me to have

Much joy, much peace, much love, much life

More of You

More energy

More freedom

Pain, care & stress free

Is what You create in me

Walking with confidence, security & knowing

A sound mind with blessings of all kinds

This season filled with milk & honey

It's frothy, smooth and flows wrinkle free

All from You

In this season

Is Your design

A vibrant coming of

Color, beauty & creativity

Showcased for all to see

So much joy You desire to give

I can't say I fully understand but I do trust in Your plan

All I must do is sit and pray and wait for You

For there is nothing You have not done for me

So much that points to You

In this space, this land, this place

You have brought me

I am ready to dive in

Just take my hand and stand close to me

I look forward to the flight & new heights

But only if You are at the center with me & my entire being

I am fragile on this course

But it is You who makes the way so I am not led astray

Under Your golden sun in this delightful

Season

BELONG

The heavens rain down
Healings of all sorts
You are near so there is no fear
But excitement in my bones & open eyes to the divine
In this life under Your palm trees
A holy union with the perfect mind
Cast away lies
Inward death
Dead to this earth
To learn of my many
Hours, minutes & seconds
Made new with You
Today a chapter
Mark & open
As I take the next step I am led with depth
In this holy union Your perfect mind
Protects at all times
All I can do is thank You
For the bones You have made new
With my each move may my bones
Always belong to You
To You I forever
Belong

ALL YOU DO

Love over

Perfection

Is what

You care to see

When I trust in You

The fear disappears and the anxiety flees

The season I am in

Is made new by You

Time to trust

When my only concern is You

Following You

Loving You

I am set free

I dwell close to You

So all must pass through You

To get to me

I must trust in the love

That surrounds me

My life is filled with Your

Goodness

So help me

Trust with my all

In You for

All You Do

All You Do

SEED

I can't do it alone

And I haven't done it alone

Your heartbeat was with Me

How do I trust?

How do I love?

Grace

You fill my space

With much grace

The love & mercy

I must have for myself

And others

Grace

Is freely given & freely received

Oh so faithful You are

You gave me a seed

Under the sun & labor of the day

It grew

Help me stand back

As You honor the seed

That grew in front of me

Help me take in the joy

And blessing of the mighty seed

You entrusted with me

For one thing I know

From You is this

Seed

ALL I DO

My strength

My helper

My main source of love

You fill me up so I can

Meet the day for all that lies before me

The strength You give is seen

It soaks deep into my bones

And makes me whole

The help You give me

Shows up in the form of truth

It casts away lies

And comforts my heart

So I can do all You've called me to

The love You give me

Sets me free

Free from others thoughts

Free from worry or doubt

Made new each day I spend with You

It's just time I need with You

To fill my tank & drive away

Up the road You have paved

For me I know I must trust

You with all I

See, do & experience

In Your hands rest the keys of

faith, courage, love, beauty & truth for

All I do

GREATER GOOD

Blessings come with perspective
Wrapped in peace
Patience for yourself and others is key
Perplexed I am
By all
You do for me
Free from worry and fear
A daily practice
Became a daily blessing
Oh how good You are to me
And this is only what I can see
In this season
The seeds
You planted in my garden
Will sprout
They will grow as I rest
And enjoy the view
The time has passed
Where I learned to sit, wait and be with
You
I have muscles of joy
And excitement for the days ahead
Because You gave me hope
As You grew this muscle
I have found that in time
You work all things out for the
Greater Good

LOOK UP

I love my time

With You

In my room

In a quiet space

Love

Peace

Joy

Is what You give me

When my cup is running low

You fill me up

You help me see

The beauty around me

And the delights that fill my life

Light the way

And help me stay

On the path

You have designed

Just for me

In time all things will come

So help me be present and patient

To what is in front of me

It is

You I trust

So let my knee bend

To You

And all

You do

As they bend

It is You

That helps me

Look Up

DELIGHT

I know now there will be seasons
Not all will last
But this one I ask to keep me awhile
As long as I have my time with You
You are responsible
You go before
The mercy and goodness, it follows after You
Under the breast, the baby rest
The Shepherd & his lambs
Here everything is best
The taste, the smell, the sight
It all delights
You bring me to meadows of rest
Beauty & Truth
My family, the members, we will grow old
New life will come & the cycle of life
Will not escape us
I can see it play before my eyes
So help me be present
Love fully & enjoy this season
Stress & worry free
Filled with family time
Love and laughs
Sunsets pool-side
Sandy mountains
Singing birds
Snuggles from little ones
Iced drinks
Limes
Palm trees
Grilled octopus & butter croissants
Not all seasons are filled with so much light
But I ask to stay awhile & bask in the rays
That lace this season, consuming so much light &
Delight

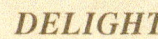

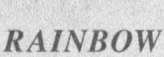

RAINBOW

After the storm You create a rainbow

You show us all things will come to pass

The rain

The sun

The warmth

The cold

The day

The night

And in the end

It's Your goodness that wins

Your sweet colors

Tenderize me

It's You who created the flood

Allowed it to pour

The beauty is You were there in the beginning

You are there at the end

It's just the journey

Learning to trust You to no end

I look up today

As the seasons have melted away

And I see the rainbow

At the end of the storm

The colors are just so beautiful

It's the cherry on top

It's the ever lasting promise

From You to man

The rainbow that appears in the clouds

For all the living

Thank You

For showing me the rainbow

That comes after the storm

May I remember all my days

To trust in You because

After the storm comes Your

Rainbow

WHO YOU ARE

Even when I don't see

You never stop

Never stop

Every promise

You have kept

I have failed You many times

And You kept no record of wrongs

Your love has never kept score

Great is Your faithfulness

My miracle worker

So much I don't see

That You do for me

My life will tell

Show the mighty love

You poured out

Into me, Your people

In my brokenness

You made me stronger

Because the cracks

Opened me for

You to fill

Healing every heart

Again and again

I believe I will see You do it

Again and again

I will worship You

All my days

Under Your glorious sun

Holy are You

Mighty are You

My Miracle worker

That is

Who You are

HEALING BALM

Deep healing is what You bring
Like an ocean wave You come washing in
And with each is balm for the wounds
Open and old, closed and new
Your people, Your women
They require healing before the move
If they move, and don't ask for the waves
The wounds grow deeper
They inflict more pain
To themselves and others
Deep healing is what we all need
Some in different ways but the truth is the same
Loved is Your creation deeply loved by You
There will always be pain in this game
But You cause one to be blameless
Before You
So we must trust in Your path
Your ways that are higher
Than our ways for it is You
Who brings deep healing
To open hearts
To closed hearts
To open bodies
To closed bodies
To women
To men
Let the waves of Your deep healing
Wash over many to help us see
Live and be
To help us move from a place
Of love from above filled with
Healing Balm

CLIMB

Slow & steady
You come in peace
You lead me down
Your path & prevent me from harm
Tender are our hearts
Strong are You
You lead and at times disguise
This love is so pure and true
Selfless all of the time
Calm & Peaceful
Your words always ring true
You slow my thoughts, heart and time
Mornings with You bring me truth
Never are they long enough
So You promise to stay by my side
Simple are Your ways
But much higher than mine
Help me to better understand
My design
My reason, my purpose, my why
As long as
You are at the center
I have reason to
Climb

OPEN EYES

How to have joy each day?
No control over others
Especially those You love
No control over much but always a choice
How to have joy each day?
When I see things through Your lens
When I only care to please You
The bliss is steady because You are steady
The love is consistent because
Your are consistent
The joy is pure because
You are pure
I see the pattern
You have never and will never fail me
So help me
Learn daily
To place my hope in You
You open my eyes
To the sunshine
Bird chirps
Banana trees
Sweet tunes
You expel the stress
That crawls toward me
I just need to be still and look to You
As You renew my sight and
Open Eyes

COCONUT MILK

It's just the start

The raw nut milk

The work, the labor

That goes into just one cup

Delicious & warm

The pulp is made thin

The juice poured out

Blended & shredded

Crafted with much effort

Creating one blissful cup

I so enjoy this cup of creamy delight

The taste is better than the rest

Might it be the effort that no one sees?

The quality?

It taste so good to me but I know no one sees

The labor that takes place behind the scenes to create

A cup fit for Kings

I praise You my love

For this raw coconut milk & the work You do in me

I know much of Your work

That takes place in me is behind the scenes

Now is the time for me to step into a season

And enjoy You & all I see

I'm grateful for this cup

You gave me

Of raw crafted coconut milk

May I always honor You

With all I do

And cherish this cup crafted with care

My coconut is Yours

Produce the milk You'd like to see in Me

I delight with this cup in my hand

Made with only the best in the land

Simple yet grand, is my

Coconut Milk

MY SIDE

The story You care to tell is one that exposes

The souls that spend time, much time with You

Their life looks different & others will be in awe

But not understand why they do what they do

As a result they will look to You because of what You do

The work in our soul, no eye has seen

The beauty in the life You create

When they were alone & no one was by their side as they cried

You told them of the beauty in the plans You had for them

You gave them something to hold on to

But what I know is even the greatest blessings

Will never bring more joy than the open eyes

To the simplicity we already have in each day

Nor will they ever compare to the quiet time with You

A muscle You needed me to have so through the fire I went

And now what is left is more divine

Kindness & peace flow

Gentle & slow

Patient & faithful

With self-control

Goodness fills the eyes of those who walk in the light

From above You watch all Your Creation

You send Your spirit where it needs to go

Some of what You see cause much joy

Others cause much pain

You know Your Creation is influenced by the unseen

A battle between good & evil

But a life that chooses You, there is no stopping all You can do

The victory lies with the soul who has many cares

You have stayed by their side

So they will tend to Your flock, in the same way You

Tend to them and this will bring glory to You

You

That will never leave

My side

UNSPEAKABLE WAYS

The time passed as I rest

Under Your wings

The prophecy

The hope

kept me still and now

New heights come You give me flight

Your wings are now mine

Higher & higher it's Your wings

I now have to soar and reach

New views there I continue to look to You

And forward to all but trust

And now know it's Your steady love

I take in each day that will never change

This is what will keep me all my days

Through the many changes

The heavy waves

The long days

The good days

The short days

Your love will fill the cracks

The brokenness is what created a way

For Your love and now I choose to stay

Peace surpassing all understanding unspeakable joy

Not always seen by the eye but felt in every breeze

Slow and steady, divine and strong

Are Your

Unspeakable Ways

HONOR YOU

Powerful is love when I experience it and lose it

I taste Your eternity through it

With love comes loss & hurt

An open heart renders

Feelings out of my control

Long nights

Restless thoughts

Loving the imperfect

Is sure to cut

Cause bleedings & sometimes beatings

But it's the closest thing

We have to eternity

Love loss shows

There is never a right time

To lose love

Its design

Is meant to last

Forever

No such thing as too soon or too late

Because it's meant to last for eternity

I want to love

What is true

So I can tell myself

It is all worth the pain

But how could I know truth without You?

So direct me to love

All that is true

Not because I fear the pain

But to

Honor You

EVERY NEED

You my One have taught me my needs
I was still & under You I rested
Day after day
Moon after moon
I looked to You
As a result
I now understand
My needs
They are simple but it's You who holds the keys
Restful nights with lots of zzz's
Gentle, quiet mornings
Peaceful, with just coffee & the sea breeze
Kindness & truth
And yummy food
Make each day new
Ocean views
Walks with You
Do just what I need them to do
Calming my mind
Centering my heart
For these things
Always lead me back to You
I understand
The importance for the soul
To rest with the divine
Because it's what carried them through
My sweet One may I always choose You
Because it's You who caters to my needs
In a way no human could ever do
No, it's just You who meets my
Every Need

MY GARDEN

A garden fountain
Locked up
A sealed fountain
A well of flowing water
The winds begin to blow
The garden is ripe
Juicy fruits that taste just right
My love is for You to choose
Ripe for the picking
Ready to taste
Making a home
Creating a space
Design from the eye
My plants watch and wait
They are ready too!
Steady, content, happy with the rays
Release the flood
Or calm the wind
The fountain is ready to
Give life again
My fountain rest
At the center of
My Garden

ONLY YOU

Patience is a virtue

And so is learning how to trust You

Not all I see, not all I feel

Not the ways of this world but You

The many ways You take care of me

Help me to see

I want to do the same for You

I want to honor You

But the ways of this world

Lead me astray

I lack faith in Your mighty ways

& it causes me to stray

It's Your path I never want to leave

My Maker, my Holy Author

Please let nothing rob the peace You give me

Keep me planted

Rooted in Your words

Your ways

Your love

Help me stay

Help me leave

To move only

When it's from You

On Your command

You are faithful

I am not

You are just

I am not

No more tossing and turning

I lay down the fight & lift up my plea

Please help me see

It's

Only You

SEAL MY LIPS

Silence my love

Honors

You

Silence can be hard to do

Still

Quiet

Hush

Not a word

A closed mouth

I leave it to

You

Wronged?

Misunderstood?

You keep me in perfect peace

As long as my mind stays on You

No need for arguments

Debate

Or controversy

My words cause trouble

So I will

Wait for You to move

&

Seal My Lips

NEXT

Only You know what's next
The who
The how
The when
And it's always better than all I expect
Faithfulness will take me far
On the road ahead
So help me trust
You
I have many questions
Help me lay them at Your feet
Then let go & believe
The best is yet to come
I trust in the hope
You plant in me
You who created me
You who tends to me
You who I love
Help me trust
You
You create far greater
Than my wildest dreams
You do not explain
Your every tendency
But I know it is only
You who knows
What is
Next

ONE

You tell me of the one
Created & formed, two from one
One to love and serve
The one that will lead my soul closer to You
The one You choose
The one where two become
One
The one I have never known
The one who runs to You too
The one that loves me true
I pray to You for only one to love
To know & hold
Just
One true one
From only
You
My
One

AWAY

The world's needs are different than the souls

The world cares to feed the flesh

The soul runs on truth, healing & love

When the soul's needs are louder than the world's...you will have both

When I drink from You I experience both

Let me tell You of all I see

Spanish tile roofs

White stucco

Arches

Egyptian candle lit lamps dangle from the ceiling

The outdoor patio wraps around

The band is free to create, sing and be

Oh the many ways

You shape my days away

Clear blue water

Desert sand

Beige mountain rocks rest at peace

Heat flowing from the sun

Time and days lost

No plans

No worries

No cares

Just You & me

Beauty and peace surrounds

Grateful, thankful I am

For the many ways You take care of me

Open eyes

Open heart

Still body

Help me soak in the paradise

You set before

Me

In this time

Away

INTERFERENCE

Plans, anxiety, interference
What are your plans for me...
The clock ticks and I have an itch
Suddenly I am consumed
With thoughts that kick
Punch and scratch
At the plans and will from above
These thoughts are not from You
Help me be still
Wait patiently
For Your spirit to give & provide the provision
I need
It is there I find rest & feel so blessed
For the yielded will
Allows Your plans to proceed
Please give me perspective
To see
Fill my heart with gratitude
For all You do
So I may stay on the divine path
Free from pain, shame, distress and
Interference

2 GENTLE LAMB

You will do it

You will do it all

Create in me a

Gentle lamb

Your logic and reason do not conform the human mind

So help me be a

Gentle lamb

I will look to

You

And not all I see because

You are just in a world that is not

I will look to

You

And not all I see

You who brings me truth, light and comfort

From above

Faithfulness to You

Will launch me

Lead my way and create a light load

So all I have to do is look to

You

Ask

You

And lay it at Your feet

You my never ending source

May my roots run deep in

Your living waters as

You create in me a

Gentle Lamb

COMFORT

Oh the ways
You comfort me
You set my mind free
Hold me close
Whisper truths
Calm my heart beat with
Your ocean waves
You create a hunger in me
Keep me steady
Rock me to sleep
Wake me early
Steady are
You among my emotions
That sway
Please keep me on
Your path
Make the math unhindered by
My disbelief
You see it's
You
Who brings me daily
Comfort

HOLY AUTHOR

The time has come

The spirit is ripe

The little body

The holy temple

Ready to be seen & pleased

The visions You gave

The joy

The peace

The love

Is here

Mighty things take time

But since You are my author

My only maker

You fill the time with

Wisdom, beauty & joy

I had to learn how to place my cares on You to be set free

Now new heights You take me

Forgiveness filling each level

For myself and others

No more past fears

You have brought me here

This new land is filled with

Milk & honey

Sweetness

Creating a childlike nature

Carefree is Your design for all Your children

Young and old

Close to You

Is where my heart is renewed

Loved and kept

My maker

My

Holy Author

KINDNESS

Oh how You delight

In kindness so true

Like a bright day

Kindness has a way

Of shining the light

Causing another's heart

To delight

Holy & Beloved

You make us

You fill hearts with compassion

Sweet kindness

Humility & patience for all

And never ending forgiveness

With You

Wisdom is the teaching of

Kindness

To others and ourselves

Our body, mind and soul

Generosity You allow

In mighty folds

Teach me more of the kindness

That flows from Your light

It is You

Who shows my life the most

Kindness

UNIQUE

All I need is my guide

To stay by my side

The souls that seek You

See Your divine works

It is theirs to hold

Because they care most to dwell close

Oh so close to You

Pure is what You create

Through Your love and quality time

You show me Your custom design,

Totally unique

Unlike anything this world has seen

Your designs bring peace, beauty, comfort & serenity

Your designs are custom to my heart

They are the perfect fit

They complete the vision

They are sculpted just for me

Please stay close to me

I love Your custom designs

I love the way You design

A life filling my thoughts and dreams

Great is Your faithfulness, never ending is Your love

Crafting designs oh so custom &

Unique

VIEW

Waiting on You
Brings resources anew
Stance from above
Provides a deep breadth in view
I hope the daily sufferings
Do not compare
To the gifts in store
And in time all
Your mighty plans will
Come to pass
Please just
Help me wait on
You to expand
My breadth of
View

KEY

Please don't let the supernatural slumber or miss me
Wake my faith, strengthen me
Create a desire to wait and praise
Wake my faith, strengthen me
I will wait for You to set me free
I will wait for Your
Mighty power to be displayed
Again & again
I want to serve You
Long enough to see
Your work set me free
Long enough to experience Your peace
It is You, Only You
I love and trust with my every do
So please, wake my faith
Move the mountain and grant me peace
I'm ready to collect
I'm ready to see
The full harvest
My mighty gardener
The planter of my dreams
My hope is in You
Nothing else
You are the only One
Who holds all the keys
Who will set me free
Help me, wake my faith
For each of Your keys
To unlock what's next & the truth of all
You promised to be
I promise to wait for
Your
Key

FOR YOU

If it's not

From You

I don't want it

The love

The life

The career

The city

The blessing

If it's not

From You

Remove the desire

With each passing wave

I now know

What is from

You

Is best

And better

I will try my hardest to abandon my

Unfaithfulness...

And choose what is

From You

For You

HOPE

There is a wait
For the
Hope
In the waiting
You give vision
Gifts
Strength
Blessings
It's well worth the wait
There is wait
In the
Hope
In the wait
Hope grows
Hope is of and from
You
The feeling of trust for the
Vast unknown & unseen
The feelings of desire and expectations
Grow for certain things
So wait for the
Hope
Before I move or do
Help me
Wait for the
Hope

ALWAYS

Always mine
Companionship of the
Most High
You make a
Home
With me
Always with me
You who comforts me
Bring the
Peace
I can not see
But feel
Deep in my bones
You who comforts me
Always

QUIET MY LIFE

Slow and steady

Present and aware

Calm and reassured

Gratitude marked by simplicity

Patience met with love

Giving where I can

Praying where I can't

Love made pure

By the lens

You create

For me

Please make my life quiet

Mark it with

Your presence

Please

Quiet my Life

POSSIBLE

"*Tell me of the impossible, My sweet child*"
What has been impossible?
Your dream school
Landing the job
Rising above death
Loving through pervasive hate
Injustice and blood shed?
Peace in the midst
Dancing in the storm
Twirling in the lions den
Using the pain to create
Death to life
Water to wine
With You by my side
Nothing has been impossible in my tiny life
Nothing...in time...that is
So help me trust once again & let go
Of all You do I do not understand
I will watch
As You again make the
Impossible
Possible

GOODNESS

There is not one desire You do not see
Or care to give Me
Help me give You everything
Trust in Your goodness
May there no longer be a stealing of peace
May it no longer flee, I know it's me
My flesh, the brokenness, it stops me from
Trusting in Your daily goodness that surrounds me
Because of Your goodness
There is not one desire, blessing or thing
You care to not give Me
And yet I am quick to forget
And hurt, pain & bitterness move in
So help me trust in Your goodness
It pours out from above
Keeps my family safe and loved
Protects the weak & shelters those in need
Goodness I do not understand but thankful I am
Goodness I do not deserve but grateful I am
Goodness that causes us to look above & trust in You
And not all we see
Let it flow, pour out on all those who seek
Trust & rest under Your wing
I might never understand but I thank You for all the
Goodness You have shown me
Faithful and true
It's You
Your goodness
Following me
Please always keep my eyes open to Your
Goodness

I CHOOSE YOU

I choose You above

Fear

Anxiety

Pride

Lust

Anger

Hurt

Calm the storm, hold my hand & walk by my side

You will set the table

Prepare the feast

And bless me beyond my wildest belief

A banquet before my enemies

The table is set

Books, rainfall, lovers & true friends,

I smell like vanilla and my fruit is no longer stolen and bitter

But renewed

Rebuilt & greater, mightier than before

Beauty that makes me glow, and land my enemy once owned

Belongs to meeeeeeeeeeeeeee

Back with the sea breeze

You will

Silence the lies

Stop my cries

Heal my scars

And soothe my mind

You will

Give me hope for the things untold

Vision for what's next

And a path to rest my each step

You will

Keep me warm

And speak to my soul

All You

Ask is that

I Choose You

FLY

You are ready
Ready to see me fly
You have seen it all
As the seasons changed
You were by my side
And strong You made me
Made new is what You say to me
Through and by Your loving hand
Now is the time
You are ready to see me fly
Wings from above
Divine
They will spread wide
And lift me high
The higher I go
The stronger they grow
They are now part of me
Connected to my spine
They will take me far and wide
They will encourage
Your design
You will lift me high
Now is the time to
Fly

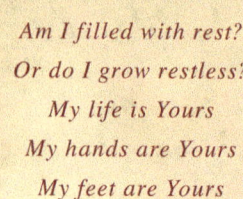

RESTFUL & RESTLESS

Am I filled with rest?

Or do I grow restless?

My life is Yours

My hands are Yours

My feet are Yours

The work of my hands and the direction of my steps

May they always be Yours

Do You call me to rest?

Do You call me to be rest less?

What's the season?

Where do You direct my steps?

What is next?

Ezer: To rescue/ To save and be strong

Now please direct my steps

As I grow in rest

As I learn what it means

To sit and wait for You

An ezer

You form me into

I know

You will show me what's next

Its

You

I know I know

You will show me which way to step

Restless is not Your design

But strong

In both seasons of

Restful & Restless

SUBMIT

A hidden will

Trials

And acceptance

In the midst of the unknown

Even in the midst of the known

I must hide in Your arms

Love I can not always see

But feel

Your will is upon me

So let it be done

All the other thoughts

Must yield

So let

Your will be done

Trust in Your love

Is what has gotten me through

Time and time again

Trusting in You

Submitting to You can be far from easy

But time and time

I learn it is what's best for me

As I learn to submit

I find myself

Walking in Your will

Which is always far greater than anything

I could have ever dreamed

So please, help me

Submit

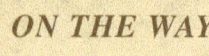

ON THE WAY

Freedom is knocking

Peace lies in the unknown

New season indeed

With it blows the winds of change

Yesssssssss

Change is finally on the way

Change is around the corner

It will bring blessings of all sorts

Tender love

Words from above

Anointed are the steps

In my calling

I walk

now RUN

Let go in love

For change is coming

Mighty and strong

The winds of change blow

Ready to explode

Allow excitement and joy

To lace my steps

Change change change

Is

On the way

SHOW ME

Show me the way
Direct my very next step
Give me the words
Or help me be silent & still
Show me the way
Direct my very next step
Please show me what is next
A fork in the road
Give me the map
I care only to
Walk along the path sown from above
So please, please
Give me peace
Direct my next step
Write the way
&
Show Me

REST

Created by You

Rest

Illuminates & transforms

Rest

Saves me from becoming enslaved

Even of what is good

Rest

A tonic for the strong

Rest

Not just when sick

Rest of the mind, soul & body

You give me

Rest, care & love

Those who walk with favor find

Rest

With trust in promises from above I have

Rest

With favor, hope & love I then can

Rest

Please bless & keep me

Let Your favor be over all I love & touch

For with you I find

Rest

HEAVENLY VIEW

All that is good comes from You

The beauty found in nature

The colors I see

So much beauty to take in daily

Why now can I see?

ohhh, how I have learned to let go

With trust most days

Because it's You that makes a way

And when my mind runs

Fills with thoughts that do not feed

It's You that sets me free

When the worry creeps in You calm me

So much to be grateful for & the best part is

I can ask You anything

I am oh so needy & tender right now

Each morning I bring all my questions & thoughts to You

Which doesn't seem to bother You

You give answers that are true

They help set me free

To live and breathe under Your sun

With views of palm trees each morning

As I bring my thoughts to You,

In time,

You renew me

Causing me to see things

From Your

Heavenly View

DESTINY

Help me

Get excited

Be excited

Moving on my behalf

Blowing the winds of change

You are creating a way

Help me

Get excited

Be excited

For what is next

Sweet, kind, and gentle

I can trust in all You have

Never would

You forget me

Please help me

Get excited

Be excited

With You I experience more of my

Destiny

BLESS ME

Cherry print nails

Citrus flavored drinks

Bread

Lemons

Limes

An entire orange

Mixed with some

Wine

Long walks and talks

Brain dumps

Quite time

Lavender and eucalyptus showers

Sunny days

Slow days

Busy days

Caffeine for days

Espresso

Cappuccino

Latte

Matcha

Tea time

Farmers market runs

Self-care to better care

Oh how You

Bless Me

LIBERATE

You do not limit
You liberate
You make a way
You carve a path
You do not limit
You liberate
You open the right door
You close the wrong
Your time
Your reason
Your rhythm
You are just
You are true
It is
You who I
Trust
You do not limit
You
Liberate

SILENCE

My silence
Will pave the way
For there are
Spiritual forces at play
Please let my prayers
Lead the way
We have all strayed from
Your ways
But I am ready to
Cooperate in
Your ways
Your purpose occurs
When I wait for
You to lead the way
Please do not delay
I am at
Your feet with
Submission that is complete
Trusting in the longed for
Answered prayers
Please, pave the way with my
Silence

SOMETHING NEW

The pressure

The squeezing

Molds

Something new

Learning how to

Put things to bed

Is protection from

You

Holding too tight

To anything that's not

You

Is what I must learn not to do

But I do

Time and time again

Sleep dwindled

Appetite suppressed

Oh please please please

Teach me to put things to bed

Let it rest

Do what only

You can do

And mold me into

Something New

CLOSE TO ME

Faithful, faithful, faithful
Blessings, blessings, blessings
Tension in my bones grows
Comfort & cove me in Your blanket of love
A legacy that does not fade
With growing age
Is the shape of ones heart
And tender ways
My soul is thirsty
But I must wait
I know
This is the last chapter
That will just be
You and me
The sun lights my path
For the world to see
The mighty mighty life
You create for
"A soul that dwells
Close to Me"

WAIT ON YOU

Help me wait on

You

The time will pass

The promises will come

Your love is enough to get me through

Help me wait on

You

You are the beginning and the end

You see and know it all

Your love will get me through

Please help me trust in only

You

It's only

You who loves me so true

It's only

You with a view from above

Help me wait on

You

What is next is from

You

As I write

You are shaving down the mountain

And carving a path

A path designed by only

You

Please please please

Help me

Wait on You

HOW IS IT SO?

How is it so?

Your foolishness

Is wiser than

The wisest of man

How is it so?

Your weakness

Is stronger than

The strength of any man

How is it so?

I always forget, time and time again

Filled with worry I grow

How is it so?

I lack trust in

Your wisdom

Your power

That is much greater than anything

I could ever do on my own

Than any combined human strength

For weakness

You do not own but

Even if so

You are far greater

Than anything

Any human

All humans

Could ever do

On their own

Foolish me!!!!!

Tell me...

How is it so?

TERRACE

Beautiful faith

A gift to

Your creation

Loving, kind, gentle and strong

You make...

Pain. Pain. Pain.

Marks my gain

Pure pure pure

Purified

You make

Through the fire

And not one burn

Made new because of

You

Now my sweet love

Is the fun part

Rain. Rain. Rain.

Down on me

And help me be

Still. Still. Still.

And listen to

You

In the dancing branches and

Warmth from the sun

Holy love flows from

Above

Please keep me still as

You rain down on me

Rain. Rain. Rain.

Is

Your

Terrace

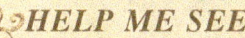

HELP ME SEE

Shame Shame Shame
On me
Oh please
Help me see all
You do for me
In the name of love
You have watched over me
Planted me by springs
And blessed me with things
I do not deserve
But do see
The love of my family
Friendships filled with care
But now all I can feel
Is all that upsets me
Oh please
Help me see
All you do for me
It's you I love
You I belong to
You who gives me life
Oh please
Help me see

TESTING

Waiting on
You can be hard to do
Very very very
Testing
But I know it is
What I must do
Simply wait on
You
You who created the heavens
Formed the Earth
And spoke commands to the sea
Will always look after me
So please
Keep me strong, faithful & whole
As I learn to
Wait on
You
The season of
Testing
Will come and go
But it is
You who gets me through
It is
You who
Guides me through the
Testing

NOT MINE

What do I have
That is not from
You...
Is it love?
Is it dreams?
Maybe my blessings?
What is it that
You can not do?
Why would I want
Anything more than
You?
What I want and hold close is
Yours
Not mine
It's
Your time
I must learn to wait on
And in the meantime
I will practice giving everything to
You
Because it's
Yours
Not mine

MY WISH

"My sweet Vendy

I wish my children learned to trust Me more

I wish many did not go their entire lives

Carrying the worry that surrounds them

With every turn

Every decision

Every change

Every stay

Every day

I wish my sweet Vendy,

My children learned to trust Me because I am good

Not like the good you have experienced on earth

No, I am good in a way that exceeds any wish, desire or dream

My goodness is not something my children understand because this
world is so far removed from Me

I wish my sweet Vendy, My children learned to trust Me

Because I have their best of everything

I have the best path for them to take and when they trust Me

I open each door and carve a path

And on that path they will start to see it

Could have only been Me

You see my sweet Vendy

I take good care of my children, old and young,

When they choose Me

My ways

My thoughts

When they place their faith in Me

I'd like my Creation to know

That the all powerful

The alpha and the omega

Sees their every need

For them to understand is

My Wish"

KINDNESS IS KING

Job well done

Is what

You say to me

For change is hard

But knowing it's from

You will empower

Me

To do all

You'd like me to

Serving well and loving fully

Will leave

No regrets because

I know it is

You who directs my each step

Time to enter a

New season

A new chapter

Filled with blessings of all sorts

But mostly more time with You

And with so many ways to go

Direction is what You give me

Never later always on time

As I prep to start this new journey

Please help me keep kindness within me

Kindness to others

Kindness to myself

Because I know

Kindness is King

COME AGAIN

So much to be

Grateful for

Help me see

The many ways

You move

Rather than all that is not

Complete

This morning

I just want to thank

You

When I do this

You help me see the many blessings

Around me

What does it take?

To live full days...

Joyful and present?

Gratitude for

You

And all

You

Do

So help me feel

Breathe

And take in

The beauty of today

For it will never

Come Again

MY FLIGHT

Above the mountain tops and city lights

Away from the daily grind and in the clouds

The sun is perched on the skyline

With blue and white

You removed me, You brought me here so I could see it is You who rules

You who plays in the sky, lights the earth and fills the moon

The divine Pilot

Allows others on my flight but

For some it's almost their time to depart

On to a different terminal they must board, but I trust You

And know it's not the end, there is a flight for each life

One with turbulence, but not for us to ever fear...my dear because

You promised I will meet all I love on the other side

My flight might be longer than those I have traveled with for 26 years

And kept by my side to warm my heart

But they must not miss their connecting flight to the other side

"It's almost time for them to join Me but I promise my sweet V

It won't be the end just a longer trip for you without them

Until you meet again, on the other side"

Sometimes...You remove Your Creation just to give us a different view

One from above so the daily worries feel small

So we feel what's important, so we release the chains, here in the sky

You want me to open my eyes here in the sky

You want me to be present and remember

The cycle of life, none can escape but all will feel

Pain, death, hope and joy will never miss a soul

"So take my hand, hold on tight You are about to fly high into the sky

Up and away you go, I just ask that You keep me by your side

Nice and tight, the dreams will arrive but not before I

Now is the time for the unseen to be revealed

with an open eyes & a beating heart

You will see and taste the beauty from your journey in the sky"

I guess it's now time to catch

My flight

LOVE ME

The ways You

Love me

With Your creation

In the sea breeze

With fluffy clouds

And blue sunny skies

Oh the mighty ways You

Love me

A warm cup in my hand

I walk

One step after another

I walk

Sweet puppies

Dancing trees

A morning FaceTime from a love

And snuggles with my babies

Oh the mighty ways You

Love me

Great is Your faithfulness to me

My eyes are not always open to

The ways You

Love me

But today I can see

I can feel

All of the mighty ways

You

Love Me

SIT & WAIT

As I

Sit & Wait

On You

I grow still, very very still

This is where I can feel the wind

Taste my coffee

Hear the waves

See the clouds

When I

Sit & Wait

I learn how to be still

That is where

(I have learned)

To hear from You

I thank You today for teaching me how to

Sit & Wait

I thank You for the ways

I have been snapped

Broken in half

If it weren't for that

I would never have made the time to

Sit & Wait

So today I ask that more souls learn to

Sit & Wait

Because that is where we get to be with

You

That is where You show us all we need to do

That is where the truth is

Cutting through the lies of the mind

Oh so much beauty

In learning how to

Sit & Wait

MY FAITH

Where do I put my faith?

What is impossible with You?

Nothing Nothing Nothing

So when the winds start to blow

Trust trust trust

Have faith in You is what I must do

I know things are not always as they seem

And as long as I am bending a knee

The protection is

Mighty Mighty Mighty

"Get ready My Dear Child

Because the army is on its way

Ready to make the way

Down from above

Oh so much noise they will create

The attacks, they are also on the way

In many different forms they will come

Strike your heart & burn your desires to the ground

but fear not for I will redeem all things"

My love from above, allow the time spent with You to get me through

Trust trust trust & guard your mind

"My sweet child You are mine

My sweet Vendela

You know well enough now

To shout my praise

And My angels will be on their way

You were made for MIGHTY MIGHTY things

So come close to Me sweet Vendela"

I will shout Your name & angels will be on their way as I

Tell tell tell the world of

My Faith

LIGHT OF MY LIFE

Longing for truth, I turn to You
Longing for hope, I seek You
Longing for light, it's with You
Oh my light for the world to see
They are hungry
They are cold
They are lost
They are troubled
You
You alone have the power
To light the world
Shine in my heart
Shine through the darkness
Your favor
Your presence
All around me
You are with me
In the morning
In the night
When I cry
When I rejoice
Now is the time
Turn on the lights
Shine shine shine
Oh it's time
You are for me
It's You
Your love & spirit
That fills me so I must do all
You have called me to do
My love, You are the
Light of My Life

AGAIN

Through the highs & lows
The crashing and the burning
The loss of breath
The pressing
The squeezing
You always find a way
Better than the last
So do it again
Today I just ask
Because of Your goodness
That it be better than the last
Now I know
My heart will forever sing
Your praise
You see
The seasons change
Love that was planted will never be uprooted
But it will leave my side
Because we all must die
Eventually there will be a time
That marks our departure
But if there is one thing
You have showed me
It's the way You move
You moved the mountains
So I believe I'll see You do it
Again and again
Time after time
You made a way
When there was no way
I will and can never forget
I'm ready to see You do it
Again

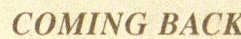

COMING BACK

Stronger, more full and better than
Greater than before
You are the One who restores
Heals
Binds wounds
And now I am
Coming back
Stronger and greater
Than before
More life
More joy
More peace
More bliss
More more more
All lies with You
Do I truly believe this?
Is it possible?
So much has changed
So much of me has changed
But
You said it
So I believe it
And wait expectantly to see
More more more
Life, excitement and joy
More more more
Dreams, love and all that is good
Oh it's
You You You
Your spirit at my back
To my side
Oh boy
I'm
Coming Back

AIR I BREATHE

Oh oh how I know

I know what it's like

My soul

To want and need

You

More than the air I breathe

Oh love

I know

I finally know

That the needs of the soul

Are far greater

In me than the needs

Of the flesh

Oh

My sweet love

I know I know

I finally know

That You are

My constant guide

It is

You

Who is by

My side

So as I begin this new season I am in

Keep and hold me close

I know

Oh how I know

My soul needs

You more than the

Air I breathe

LAND & SEA

Tell me what do you see?

I see carefree waves brushing over rocks

Sunshine highlighting the land

That sits above the resting rocks

I see homes anchored in the land & a sea that surrounds

Might this be the same sea

That He once walked on...?

Tell me what do you see?

I see clouds hovering in the sky

Looking over the land & Sea

Might these be the same clouds

That He once lived under?

What is it you'd like me to know

About my time spent on the

Land & Sea?

Oh yesss

You put it here for them and me

For all Your creation to be

To live and laugh

Love and play

Work and cry

Bask in the sun

That tends to both the

Land & Sea

Oh yesss I can now see

You planted each of us here for a limited time

Some days we just don't know why

Others the fire burns in our insides

So might the key to living our best life on Your

Land & Sea

Rest with You

The One, only One

Who could have possibly created the

Land & Sea

KEYS

Dear Maker

Of my sanctified dreams

This city

Place

You have positioned me

You are getting ready to deliver the

Keys

Yes

Keys to the city

Why now? How? What is it You want to do?

Show the world what a bent knee can do?

A knee bent to the Most High changes everything

Yes this city, desert land that meets the sea

Holds many

Keys

Keys

You will now deliver to me

Why? Is it really due to the knee that bent in the midst of all

She could not see but trusted in her move... that it was You

behind, to the side, in front and in her?

Is it really due to the knee?

That will now cause the world to see

The power in the Mighty hand

The divine who paints our lives

If we, if only we can just learn to

Bend a knee to He then comes the

Keys

RIPPLES

Ripples

In the water make noise

Ripples

In the water create waves

Some smooth as day others crash like thunder

Ripples

In life cause me to look up at You

Ripples will always be

There is no such thing as a body of water without them

Ripples are part of the master design

I am learning of the great beauty Your ripples cause

In the sea of life

They have taught me to hold on to all things

Much more loosely because surrender for us all is key

They have taught me You are in control...even of the wind

Who has no master so trusting

Who is in control will bring me much peace

They have taught me of the power in pain

And things not going my way

It created more room for You

They have taught me

To feel because

Some seasons will be better than others

And if we don't feel

We'd never know the difference

I'm thankful, oh so grateful for the sweet

Ripples

That flow

They give

Add to life in a way that has caused me to see

Opened my eyes and grew me

Thank you for my sea of

Ripples

PUMPKIN SPICE

It's the season
Of shifting leaves
Crisp mornings
And pumpkin spice lattes
Oh a season
You created
Filled with many joys
How good
You are to me
Tis the season
Of round orange squash
Pumpkins, spices and cider that delights
Tis the season
Sweet season of falling leaves
Yes yes yes
I know now to pay close attention
To the simple things
My collection of candles
Fills the room
Pumpkin spice
My scent of choice
Drifting through the air
You remind me
Of the simple joys
The fall season brings
So today I take delight
In the simple scent of the clove streaming from my latte
Oh how I love this
Pumpkin Spice

SEE LIKE YOU

I see odds

I see risk

I see greener grass on the other side

I see grand mountains

Help me to trust

Help me to

See like You

You see the beginning and the end

You see the path

You see the how

You see the possibilities

My thoughts so limited

My ways lack much faith

Oh how I long, I need to

See like You

As You prepare to do

What only You can do

Make the impossible possible

Help me to trust

Help me to

See Like You

SOOTHE MIND

Calm heart
Soothe mind
Is what You give me
Do I step right, left or stay put
Do I speak or retreat
Do I hold on or let go
So many ways to go
Calm heart
Soothe mind
Is what You give me
Not always easy
Not always clear
But peace to move where
You'd like me
Is all I need
Calm heart
Soothe mind
With these things
Nothing can stop me
So please, please, please
Continue to do
What only
You can do
Work in me a
Calm heart
Soothe Mind

SEEM

"Trust Me sweet V & not all you see"
The squares on the feed appear to be...
But the truth is things are not always as they seem
If it is not You who is steering the ship
If the equation leaves You out
It will never lead to fullness
Things are not always as they seem
You see it's easy to do as I please
And harder to trust You
Faith and trust are muscles
The more I use them
The stronger they grow
The stronger I grow
And start to see that I was created
Designed
To live carefree
Things are not always as they seem
You tell me this
Not so I can take pleasure
In ways that only serve me
But You tell me this
So I have a view that is true
One I can hang on to
A view that keeps
Me trusting and choosing You
The Instagram squares
The exterior success
Has stories behind
Ones that don't always appear as I see
Ones that aren't always as they
Seem

FORGIVE

Innocent and pure
Yet unforgiveness dwells close
Thick and strong the chains
Around my heart will grow
If I don't let go
Help me place it all in
Your hands
Please, show me how to hand it over to
You
I know unforgiveness blocks love
Please, help me let go
Why do I doubt...
Have You not always taken care of me?
Have You not always comforted me?
Have You not always made a way?
Have You not always lifted me high
And made all things right?
You will be my reason to forgive
You are enough
Your promises are enough
Your love is enough
Please help me
Forgive

MEMORIES

Minutes to hours

Hours to days

Days to years

Suns to moons

The moments pass by

Slip through my hands

So quickly they move

Leaving me with nothing but memories

I do not know what tomorrow will bring

But I thank You for memories that plant love in me

I will not always have them

Some will stay, some will go

And only You know the time

But the memories are gifts

Gifts I will always cherish

Gifts from You

I unwrap these gifts to find

There is no end to Your time

You keep me present

Make a way for me to be free

Open my eyes to the sunshine

The warmth that surrounds me

Delicious biscuits

Butter & Honey

Champagne bubbles

Hugs & laughs

The joy flowing out

From my insides

For the memories You give me

For these I will always have

The memories will get me through the night

The dark will come but I will always hold tight

To the moments and memories with those I have

I wish only for these, many more moments &

Memories

LIGHT IN ME

The

Light in me

Went out you see

My eyes lost their twinkle

My hopes and dreams buried

My spirit faded and gone was my taste

The

Light In me

Went out you see

The pep in my step

The joy that once filled my mind

Was crushed, crushed, crushed

And out went the lights with all its delights

Empty and broken I sat, waiting for You to comfort me

Night after night You held me

I chose You and out flowed streams of healing & with time

The light in me

Turned back on you see

Yours ways, time, reason, and rhyme

I will never fully understand

But because of the way You held me

My heart will always be Yours and because of this

The

Light In me

Was reignited you see

So I just tell the world

Of Your love because of what it did for me

Please comfort most broken hearts, especially the women and children

Because it is the way life flows

The babies they make and take care of will change the future

Bright bright bright will be the light

If we can just in return take care of them

So thank You again for rekindling the

Light in Me

ALWAYS BE ME

It's

You

You who parted the sea

Carried me

Adores me

Speaks to me

There is nothing

You

Have not done for me

Forever I will dwell close to

You

Forever I will love

You

Forever I will choose

You

Forever is not enough time with

You

I now know it's always been

You

Always been

You

Who got me through

"My sweet V, it will

Always be Me"

YOU DO

I have no choice but to wait on You

I see what

You do

You answer my request by guarding my ways

Placing me so I have no choice

But to lean on You for my every move

Ohhhh I see what

You do

I'm growing lonely

Hopeful and excited for all that's ahead

But lonely

So I will need You to comfort me

Or else I may choose something that's not of You

Keep me, fuel me so I can keep going

Bless my each step

Because it's for You

Whisper to my heart

What it needs to hear

You know this

More than my heart does

And when I'm sad, speak to my soul

Tell it what it needs to feel

And when I'm confused

Wipe away the mist

By opening my mind to all

You do

And when my little heart aches

Due to all I see and don't believe

Give me eyes to see all from

Your view

Ohhhhh I see what

You Do

DO GOOD

I know what You'd like from me

To do good

To do right by others

Honor

Especially those who belong to You

The family of believers

You say if we do not give up

Or grow tired of

Doing good

On Your time

We will reap a harvest

But in this situation

I'm growing weary

I do not have a heart or desire to

Do good

But rather

Be free

I feel even

The opportunity to

Do good

Is what haunts me

I hate how this world

Hurts me

Corruption is what I see!!

Please show me how to

Do good

So I can honor

You

And I know

Your will is to always honor me

I also know

It's the desire of

Your pure heart to see me

Do Good

HANDIWORK

Look what You created
How could I ever doubt You
Your power is painted in the sky
With the burning stars
The bright sun
The round moon
The vast sea & mountain tops
It's here in Your Creation
Where I see, I feel the power of Your
Handiwork
Then I head back to my room
Start my day
And doubt overcomes me
Maybe the key
Is to recall what I have just seen, witnessed in the sky, Your
Handiwork
Not done by man but done by the one who dwells above
So when I start to doubt
Please remind me of Your
Handiwork
Constantly on display for the world to see
Help me look up to the sky
Or out at the sea
There I am able to reset
And reach higher than my
Wildest dreams
Because it's Your
Handiwork
That inspires me
It points to things much greater than me
Continue to remind me of Your power and beauty
Your hand moving in my life
As I enjoy the view of Your
Handiwork

TRUST YOU

I will never understand
Why certain things happen
Take place in this world
And it will only
Rob me of my peace
The more I try to make sense of
All I see
If I can just learn to
Trust You
Believe in
Your good and true nature
I will always have peace
The why is not always what I need
But always what I want
It's the release of all that could be
It's the surrender to You
That creates room
Freedom for You to
Paint and create
A life beyond
My wildest dreams
I need to stop with the why
It's not for me
It's trusting in You
That is all
I will ever
Truly need
The weekend on the horizon brings
Soft sunsets and fresh air
And more quiet time with You
It keeps my worrying at bay
Stops the why
So I can just be and
Trust You

NEXT

The days will pass
The moons will turn
The sun will dance and smile on me
The winds will continue to blow and
The rain will pour
But it is You who will get me through
The start of something new is here
With it comes hope and joy
The excitement and peace brings bliss anew
The long days, hours, and weeks
Passed and turned into months and years
I have seen it was always You by me
The time did pass and the pain did not last
Grateful I am for all You have brought me through
Ready and full of joy I am
For the new
The people, the faces, the words, the memories
Have all shaped me
Grateful I am
Hopeful I am
And ready to move
Hold me
Bless me
And send me off
Strong
You have made me
Hopeful and trusting I am because it is
You who has seen me through
You who has loved me through it all
Held my heart and kept me going
Now send me off and hold me close
Ready I am for all that's
Next

TRY TO

Oh how much more
You desire for me
You speak
I hear
But I lack faith that activates
You promise
And I am quick to forget
You then do
I see
And question
You and
Your every move!
There is no pleasing me
Of such little faith
So my Lord
What must we do?
How do I move forward
In a way that delights You?
"Sweet V
Keep faith and lace it with every step
Keep hope in your every move
Keep love at the center of everything you do "
That's it
I will do just as
You say
Or...
Try to

RISE

The birds chirp
So early
They giggle and sing
Outside my morning window
The trees dance in the ocean breeze
The palms touch
And provide a beautiful view
For today is laced with more blessings
True in their simplicity
My cup is warm this morning
And fills my tummy
The coconut milk is raw
The coffee is fresh
My robe is cozy
And warms my flesh
My thoughts run free
Then You enter & transform Me
And all I see
Hope, vision & awareness
Is what You give me
Enough for the day is all I need
Today I will rise & work with joy
Because it is You Who is with Me
At my side ready for the ride
I very much enjoy when my love for
You is at the center of me
And wraps around all I do & see
With You by my side
Today I will
Rise

CHANGE

It hurts

It's uncomfortable

Makes you question...

Change

Brings a new lens

Different challenges

Growing pains

Change

I don't like it

I think I might actually hate it

But my soul was ready

Change

Will always take place

No matter the season

Learning to move with it

Will always be the challenge

Dear change, I welcome you

Because He is forever by my side

I will accept the change

The change from above that

Helps me see and feel & opens my eyes to what's real

Oh change

You are no longer feared

But welcomed here.

With every bend I will trust

Please help me trust

All you blow into and out of my life

Help me accept the change because I know

Nothing remains the same except for You

Your love

So I will welcome

Your

Change

RIGHT

"Keep doing Vendela what you know is

Right

This does not always mean you turn right

I might call you to turn left

The left turn might be unexpected

Unconventional, seeming impossible

But that's usually how I move

Needing you to lean on Me

Keep doing Vendela

What you know is

Right

And my ways will give you strength to fight the hidden battle

This world falls victim to daily

Keep doing Vendela

What you know is

Right

And I, the never changing & ever lasting

Will do what is

Right

By you

Keep doing Vendela

What you know is

Right

By choosing Me in little and big ways

A fruit filled life is what I give you"

Right is not always easy to do

Especially when I see the fruits that appear just as tasty

For not doing what is right

But because I seek and You speak

I must do what I know is

Right

by You

Just keep directing me, oh please, keep showing me the way

What is...

Right

COMING SOON...

ATTACKS ON THE HEART

OUT OF THE DESERT

LIFE, WHAT I LIKE

OTHER BOOKS BY VENDELA

KEYS FROM HEAVEN

378 Devotionals to Unlock Your Calling

Vendela delights in time with loved ones and finds
creativity in cooking & the sea breeze.
Follow her on Instagram @VendelaRaquel or visit
www.vendelaraquel.com